CROWN OF WILD

Erica Bodwell

Winner of the Two Sylvias Press Wilder Prize

Two Sylvias Press

Two Sylvias Press
PO Box 1524
Kingston, WA 98346
twosylviaspress@gmail.com

Cover Artist: Menashe Sofer
Cover Design: Kelli Russell Agodon
Cover Photo Credit: Monica Justesen
Book Design: Annette Spaulding-Convy
Title Page & Interior Bio Art: Erica Bodwell
Author Photo: Monica Justesen

Created with the belief that great writing is good for the world, Two Sylvias Press mixes modern technology, classic style, and literary intellect with an eco-friendly heart. We draw our inspiration from the poetic literary talent of Sylvia Plath and the editorial business sense of Sylvia Beach. We are an independent press dedicated to publishing the exceptional voices of writers.

For more information about Two Sylvias Press please visit:
www.twosylviaspress.com

First Edition. Created in the United States of America.

ISBN: 978-1-948767-09-5

Two Sylvias Press
www.twosylviaspress.com

Praise for *Crown of Wild*

"What is the sound of in ruins, broken?" In Erica Bodwell's striking debut, brokenness is inflected with pain and also with beauty. Bodwell knows how humans get damaged and do damage, and sticks close to the stressed and womanly body: its sensations, its pressures, what impinges on it, how it breaks free—or how it can't. Her sounds are dense and vivid, her characters in these formally-varied lyric narratives are as real as characters in short stories. This is a book I'll keep coming back to.
— **Daisy Fried**

ક૭

In Erica Bodwell's Crown of Wild, there are many kinds of wildness. There is the wildness, for instance, found in a young woman's coming of age, her discovery of both desires and betrayals along the way. There is also the ugly wildness of the pervasive violence against women, especially sexual violence, within the family and in the world beyond. But there is another kind of wildness at work within all these poems. At every turn, this poet sizes up her world for both its menace and its occasional but fleeting beauty. With razor-sharp diction and stunningly original associations, Bodwell's poems show us that becoming a whole person does not happen by accident. It requires courage, resilience, and, in this case, an unflinching intelligence. These strengths bring the poet to what she calls her own "bright freedom." Such freedom is an authentic and durable "crown of wild," and this book is its story. — **Fred Marchant**

ક૭

Can a book of poetry be sexy and sad at the same time? It can if its speaker is inquisitive enough. If she's wide-ranging and empathetic and forgiving and observant enough. This book of American womanhood rises out of a sensually-grounded tension between "wildish things" like our speaker's "tresses [like a] nest of milky way & glitter-grouse" and real dangers that lock her into "white-hot needles [of] navy narcotic / oceans" or imaginings of real-world slayings and other sins. Crown of Wild is a street-wise "long waltz with the night" grounded in smart mournful tones. But it does not once give in to self-pity or regret. In fact, Crown of Wild is a joyful book, taking its pleasures out of the redemptive possibilities of both language and life. The lament here is real, but so is the frolic and play. And that's why you should read it and will love it. — **Adrian Blevins**

Acknowledgements

Gratitude to the following journals, in which these poems, or earlier versions, appeared or are forthcoming:

Alyss, "Aubade in Which the Wolf Wakes Me Up," as "Conversation with the Wolf"

Apiary, "Make a Law That Loves the One Who Breaks It"

Barnstorm, "Cadet"

Beloit, "Flake"

Coal Hill Review, "Camp, 1979"

Crab Fat, "Starry Messenger"

HeART, "Aubade in Which an Angel is Present"

Hot Metal Bridge, "The Girl in the Bed"

Indolent Books, "Physics Lesson for Those in Despair"

Inkwell, "Aubade in Which I Awaken"

Litbreak, "Every Sentient Being"

Mom Egg Review, "Child, Mother"

The North American Review, "Inventory" and "Praise Planet: Galactic Ballet"

PANK, "All the Stories I Ever Told Myself"

Persephone's Daughters, "Accident" and "Summertime"

r.kv.ry, "Aubade in Which Grace Appears"

Stone Highway Review, "To the River"

The Tishman Review, "Match" and "Forest Aubade"

Unearthed, "Authentic Presence"

Whiskey Island, "I Cut My Long Hair"

White Stag, "Torch Song for Kayla Mueller," as "Torch Song for the Badass"

"Leap," "Summertime," "Camp, 1979," "The Girl in the Bed," "Were This the House," "Ode to the Yellow Sparkle Snare Drum," "Accident," "Dear Kayla, What Was It Like," and "Aubade in Which a Memory Appears" appeared in the chapbook, *Up Liberty Street* (Finishing Line 2017).

Many thanks to the Fine Arts Work Center in Provincetown, MA, where I have been attending summer workshops since 1997, and to the Colrain Poetry Manuscript Conference, without which this book would not have come together. Thanks also to the Tupelo Press 30/30 Project, Mass Poetry and the Massachusetts Poetry Festival, the New Hampshire Writers Project, the Kimball-Jenkins School of Art, the New Hampshire Institute of Art and the Maine College of Art for providing opportunities to work with great poets and artists outside the MFA.

Immense gratitude to my poetry teachers: Patricia Fargnoli, Toi Derricotte, Daisy Fried, Ada Limón, Nick Flynn, Terrance Hayes, Rowan Ricardo Smith and the exquisitely generous Fred Marchant. Special shout-out to Rachel Zucker and the *Commonplace* podcast for the brilliant interviews with poets and others on craft, subject matter, the artistic life and more. I have found so many poets and learned so much just listening.

To Kelli Russell Agodon and Annette Spaulding-Convy of Two Sylvias Press, thank you for your prompts, your inspiration, your tarot cards and your belief in and championing of women writers. Thanks most especially for believing in *Crown of Wild* and giving it a home in the world. And to Adrian Blevins, it's an honor to follow you as winner of the Wilder Prize.

Thanks to Kellie Wardman for 25 years of writing-best-friend-sisterhood, and Meagan Quinn and Emari DiGorgio for all manner of poetry partnership, editing, "po-biz" advice and support.

Gratitude and grace and so much love to Gail DiMaggio, my writing partner, who has seen and commented on every poem I've written, every drawing I've made and every painting I've painted since we met eight years ago. Here's to books & Paris & dogs & Buddha.

Love and light to Jordan and Matthew—there's nothing better than seeing one of you typing away in my writing room.

And to A—

Table of Contents

For Matthew and Jordan,
who taught me how to be less careless with my life.

But I didn't die. I went right
back the next day, but in a t-shirt
and didn't try to be pretty, just
swam like something ordinary,
something worthy of the sea.

—Ada Limón

I

Blessed

You too might, in the most God-awful hour
of your life, allow a man
you meet at the gas station
to nibble your neck and stroke your hair
with his rust-covered hands.
If he does, draw him close,
let the desperate press of his thighs
pray through your jeans.
Take off your shirt
and grab his lank hair in hunks
as he tells you his sad story
of flannel and winter; feed him
half the glazed donut you bought, and receive
the blackout of him
as he lays you down in his gravel-strewn truck-bed,
gently as a nuzzling lamb,
with no force at all.

Dear Tim, I Release You

Thirty years ago, towering bonfire throwing sparks
high in the air. In an adjoining field,

John Danner pins me to dirt, roots press my spine.
He'd pulled me from the heat,

led me through the woods—I had looked back,
smiled. Chosen. Did I mind the rough brush

of his lips, his mouth in my hair?
And when he let his full weight drop, knocking

air from my lungs, I saw Orion—his bow,
his arrow—standing triumphant overhead. From there,

I located Pleiades, the Big Dipper,
myself. It was then the amber hardened

and with it you, Tim—
you. Another star fixed fast in my dark sky.

Aubade in Which I Awaken

Like a Glock
& a dare, a blizzard-stranded
Honda, a constellation
of bite-marks
across a collarbone,
being lost
in the worst neighborhood
in Syracuse,
like thirty-six stitches
in a gaping palm,
playing quarters
with Stolis
in the Moscow dawn, eyelids
stuck shut
with slept-in mascara,
like leaping
from a rusted
train trestle, praying
to Venus
& not the virgin, dragging
a metal detector
over morning's fresh sand
& pocketing every
unearthed thing—
what did I think I'd find out there,
blindfolded, accepting
all suitors,
in my long waltz
with the night?

Leap

Cement wall. The girl's feet just off the edge. Midair, she touches nothing. His outstretched arms, her small body. Black bangs cut across her forehead, his Roman nose in profile, his smiling mouth. Mittens dangle from a red string that gets tangled when she, with great concentration, spreads her coat on the floor, slips her arms in and flips it over her head. He wears black leather gloves. Do his hands still carry a scent of cowhide, when, in the middle of the night, he covers her eyes?

Dear Kayla, Did You Pray
—after Kayla Mueller

For each month's blood, all those months
in captivity—did the unseen moon keep track?
Did the warm liquid rush ease you from sleep,
did the blood bring reprieve?

In captivity, did the moon light your dreams?
Did a scabbed leather boot kick you awake,
did the moon bring reprieve,
did they take you to him?

When black steel shoved you awake,
did you point to the sheet, crimson stain,
bright blood? Did they take you to him,
did he send you away, unclean,

spared—did you sleep on stained sheets,
did you dream? The next night,
when they brought you, unclean, to him,
did you cry, did you pray?

Did you dream, through the pain—
did the moon lift you up, did she answer
your star-laced prayers,
did you go to her, did you stay?

Did you drift up to her, when he pushed into you,
did the moon hide you away in her mountains?
Kayla, it's okay, you can stay all night
in her cool and powdery folds.

When she gathered you into her silvery peaks,
did you thank her for blood
and the tides? Did her touch brush your face,
did you look down on him, did you pray?

I Cut My Long Hair

i cut   my long hair   cut summer

        wild away   tangled within i found

      remnants of burned-out stars   lone starling & some

leftover mosquitoes   i cut

     my long   hair it was time

              to put away   wildish things

       no longer

   could i pile heaps of hair on top of my head

        crown of wild   crown of feral

         i stopped

    washing myself   clean in streams blueberries

  shriveled   on the bush

         soap & razors

steel & plastic   i gathered tresses

      nest of milky way & glitter   grouse

   feather small cairn   i swept the nest

  from the house   i abandoned   my wild

         i locked   the door

II

Summertime

n. 1. *Female.* As in sleepaway camp, as in sleeping away, away from
_____, as in blue, as in moon, as in lake's edge, silvery. 2. *Warm.* As in
open windows, as in neighbors can hear and who cares. 3. *Water.* As in
swim the length of every pool, breath-holding, as in rising, as in standing
one-legged in the sea, as in wave, as in under. 4. *Free.* As in purple
sparkle banana seat, as in gift from _____, as in grownups shitfaced on
sangria, as in French kissing Matt Matera, Milky Way's chalky smear, as in
light pollution. 5. *Sun.* As in star, as in slathered baby oil, crisscrossed tan
lines, as in solar system, Andromeda, universe. 6. *Light.* As in sunrise, as in
tiptoe outside, toenails shimmering with dew, as in being put to bed while
it's still. 8. *Station Wagon.* As in yellow, as in emissions, as in climate
change, as in half-mile of beach, disappeared. 9. *Refugee.* As in stranded,
as in sinking, as in sleep away camp over, as in can't go home. 10. *Done.*
As in Earth turning on its axis, orbiting its star, as in bright face of
Americas spun away from the sun, as in lightless, as in frozen ground,
_____ returning, as in January.

Camp, 1979

She sits on the splintered wooden steps, alone. The smell of wet canvas
Mixes with a breeze off the lake. Behind her, six cots,

Striped mattresses cottony and thick. She lays out her plaid sleeping bag,
Dislodges a scab and brings it to her mouth, watches them retreat:

Mother, stepfather, stray younger siblings. Her little sister's hair
Flies up and a tiny butterfly barrette drops to the dirt. Flat on her back

On the slatted platform she stares at cobwebs lacing the peaked frame,
Seeping beads of dew, dark speckles of mold. A daddy longlegs

Walks across her thighs. She considers pinching him up by one leg
And chucking him out the back as she will hundreds of times that month

At the request of squealing tent-mates. Soon the lunch gong will ring and
She'll stand, grind the barrette into the ground with her heel, take her seat

In the dining hall, wake at midnight for a starry swim.
She lets him move along.

The Girl in the Bed

wants a witness, other than that girl in the doorway, lounging, rolling a Tootsie pop around in her mouth, looking through the bed-girl to the pop-up camper in the backyard, wings spread as if for liftoff, exhaling its winter must. A witness to last summer, to her body crammed into wing's mildewed apex, screen's mathematical squares imprinted on her cheek, hand that moved deliberately across the flannel sleeping bag unzipped to lie flat. A witness other than that doorway girl rolling her eyes, clicking her lollipop, who rose from the bed-girl's body and hovered on the aluminum ceiling, refusing to throw even a glance at the figure lying stock-still on the thin mattress, as if she were textile, furry, made for touching.

Were This the House

Where my parallel self slept,
Where I'd sketch in three older brothers
To stand watch like German Shepherds—
She and I would face each other

Cross-legged on the plush rug,
She holding the soiled yarn taut,
Ponytail winding its end into her mouth,
Me threading my fingers

Through crisscrossed lattice,
Our foreheads touching in concentration,
Pyramid of stacked jacks waiting
For her to fly

Through onesies, twosies,
Her silver bracelets scraping the wood
In metronomic time—
Were this that twinned world,

Were I ever able to meet that girl
Who walks with me, hand-in-hand, in my dreams,
The sun would throw back its face and laugh.
A plate of cookies would appear at our feet.

Ode to the Yellow Sparkle Snare Drum

Power sparkler, noise maker,
Percussive silencer of sisters. I'll stand on tiptoes

To pound you, slam you, slap you, tighten
Your tension rods, snap your snare head.

I'll carry sticks hard and long
For you. You saved me

From the flute and its case like a doll's casket,
From tiny boxes of thin reeds that splinter like envy,

From white plastic chairs in the wind section.
Silver-circled dazzler, I'll snap my sticks into the clip

Screwed to your hoop, slide you into the plush red
Of your slick hard case, keep you

From dust & snakes. O yellow sparkle snare drum, thank you
For giving me a reason to walk with weapons.

Dear Beauty Editor

Dear Beauty Editor:

I tried the sugar scrub. I put a glass jar next to the sink and every night I scoop crystals into my palm and rub my hands together. I say the words in Issue 12: "Believe it and you will become it". I taste sweetness while I buff away the layers of my face. I don't think it's working—there are still shadows on my bedroom wall and one time, the jar shattered when I picked it up and I got five stitches in my palm. What else can I try?

ℰ

Dear Beauty Editor:

Don't tell anyone, but even though I'm 11 and a half, I still go to the library every day in the summer. In the morning I go to swimming lessons in the Hudson River—I passed my Advanced Swimmer test today. The current was really strong. I know I will be a lifeguard in a few years and I'll wear a red one-piece with high cut legs, twirl my whistle and everyone will look at me. But for now, I still go to the library. They let me come in with bare feet and wet hair! I haven't used my curling iron all summer. I know you think I should. The library has an old claw foot bathtub lined with carpet samples. It's like a padded patchwork quilt. I lie in there and read all afternoon. I think the librarian thinks I'm a boy.

ℰ

Dear Beauty Editor:

Have I told you about the lake? I'm at camp for a month and there are no mirrors here. I hope I still look okay. We sleep in tents on platforms and at night take aluminum canoes out on the water. They are still warm from baking in the sun all day. When I sink down into the canoe's belly, I feel like the sun saved some of its heat just for me. I wanted to tell you that my friend French braided my hair and she said it looked really good.

℘

Dear Beauty Editor:

I tried to do my hair like you told me to. I tore an old t-shirt into strips. I had your step-by-step instructions. I COULD NOT DO IT. I tried for 3 hours but the strips kept falling out. Just to let you know, I won't have the "windswept-at-the-beach" look without more help. I keep trying to take your advice. You know, I don't even care if I'm the best me I can be. I want to be another girl altogether. Do you think I need rag-curled hair for sure?

Accident

It happened at least once a year, ER doors
Slid open. Her lip her chin her knee her palm,
Here comes another one. Nurse's sigh
Was gentle.

ER doors slid open. Bloodied towel—
Child's testament. Nurse's voice
Hushed penumbra, doctor's lamp seared
Apple flesh, cleaved wide.

A girl, bloodied towel. Her mother
Said, *I had no idea.* Sun-bright, silver needle
Stitched ragged flesh, split open. Mother
Said, *sorry, sorry.*

Mother wept, *I didn't believe her.* Girl drifted
On narcotic waves. Mother
On the phone, *sorry, sorry. You know, you know,
She's accident prone.*

Girl dreamed white-hot needles, floated navy narcotic
Oceans. Mother, insistent, *I had no idea.*
Girl, prophecy. *Accident prone.* It happened
At least once a year.

Things Said to a Teenage Girl at the Dojo

Always use your opponent's weight against him.
You look fat, we're going to call you "Fat Chance".
Let him fall into you, then step aside.
I can give you a ride home.
Here's how to fall.
Word around the club is you're a virgin.
Just let yourself crumple.
Wash your feet! You're disgusting.
You're definitely Olympics material, if you drop two weight classes.
Hop up into my arms.
You can work out with the adults if you like.
Use your forearms to smack the mat.
I'll hold you upside down from the knees—50 sit ups, now!
We're having a party. You're the only junior invited.
You mean to tell me you can't double-jump?
Just inhale and resist the urge to cough.
Barbara is such a bitch. Never get married.
Want to hear a joke?
Did Tommy put those bruises on your thigh?
How do you make a whore moan?
Take your hands off that apple.
Don't pay her.
Barbara's going to visit her sister in Puerto Rico.
I'll teach you arm bars but don't tell anyone—it's illegal.
You need to put in some extra training time.
How the hell did you gain 8 pounds in 5 days?
Here, pull these Sudafed capsules apart and chew them.
I made you. I can unmake you.

Dear Kayla, Did You Sleep

Kayla, in captivity, did you sleep?
Did the pale Aleppo moon track your nights?
When the AR-15 nudged you awake,
did your God hold your hand,

was it night?
When the key turned in the lock,
did God open His arms
to the girls in their terror?

When the bolt slammed
into place, did you pull them in close?
Did you cradle their fear, Kayla,
smooth tangled hair?

Did you pull them in close
through long desert days,
did you teach them to French braid,
to spell out their names

in the dusty, desert-sand floor?
On the night they escaped,
did your prayers carry their names
to the moon, shining cold

overhead? The night they escaped,
did you choose not to leave?
Did you promise the moon—you'd stay
if she'd light their way?

When you chose not to go,
did your God hold your hand?
Did the moon sing
in your dreams, did you sleep?

III

Aubade in Which the Wolf Wakes Me Up

The wolf's whispering smack
In my ear, taunting, *Come on. Just one more*
Line, one more one more one more…

Look, the wolf says, at those cheekbones.
You're sitting on your hands
To keep from touching him.
What's one walk in the woods?

Don't you want a trip
To the hexagonal blue blueness, a thwack or two
Of the rubber band

At your wrist? Those razored cuts
Above your knee
Are so hot. Come on! Just one
One one one one —

Back and back it comes, sleek-coated,
Shimmering. Lips curled, teeth bared. It comes
And comes and comes. O wolf

O desire o god of craving won't you please
Curl up and sleep? Sure, the wolf says,
Anything you want.

And So the Dance Began

First came Matt color in his cheeks
And so the dance began
Thirteenth summer French kissing by the pool
Overhead stars were spinning

And so the dance began
David appeared, crown of curly hair
Overhead, stars were grinning
Concrete warm, our bare feet touching

Geoff stepped in, smoldering, older
Taste of pot on his breath
He left wet footprints on concrete
Hollow at his throat called to me

Taste of Stolis on his breath
Simon waltzed in, taller than my brother
My forehead just brushed his throat
He sent me twirling across the yard

Then came Jimmy, with a car
Exhaust and chlorine in the air
We held each other, swaying in the yard
It was then I started falling

Smell of chlorine and cut grass in the air
Home from college, Mike appeared
Free falling, I grabbed for his shirttail
The sun rose over the fence

Summer before college, alone on the chaise
Sun-warmed chorine stung my eyes
I reached for Matt, Mike, Jimmy, Geoff—
And so the dance began

Tel Aviv

twenty   desert   my most alone summer
I sat in a café   ate a slice of honey cake
a soldier stood on the corner   sunglasses propped
on angled cheekbones   he leaned against a mural

etched in concrete   sun-tipped bathers lounged
frozen in white paint   salt in the air
and on the tongue   there was a sadness
everywhere present   sticky crumbs

filled my mouth   the soldier
removed his glasses   I went to him   he wore
a Galil sash   his apartment was sparse
he broke chocolate into pieces   sweet smears

on sheets and my tongue   he begged me
to stay cried out   when he came   his olive skin
matched mine   we looked like twins
the rifle slept on the floor   when we fucked

he murmured in Arabic   I cried when I said
I can't stay   he brought flowers
to the airport   there was a sadness
everywhere present

The Body Keeps the Score

As if in a dream, the body keeps the score—
Nurse says, *You have to relax, dear.* Does he know,
the one who leaned in the doorway?
My prayer goes here.

Nurse says, *Relax or it won't work.* Doctor
shakes his head, *You college girls.* Slides a needle
in my arm. My prayers narcotic dreams—
would the boy say, *sorry, sorry*, would he stroke my hair?

We college girls are so wild. At sea with vodka, sex
and prayers—would he recall
my name? Dream: he holds my hand. Nurse says,
ok, it's done. Prick of blood where needle was,

my prayer he never knows. Walking campus
in a dream, vodka goes down easy.
It's done, I'm back to one.
Familiar pain where a body was,

Like a dream, the trees are greening. Summer
and I'll leave this place. Doctor said, *Be careful.*
My grief my twin that walks with me,
the body keeps the score.

Summer of the Braid

junior summer   two of us alone   in the lab   long days
twirling   on stools   waiting   for electrons

to switch places   with electrons   come with wet hair
she said   not washed   just wet   she tipped

way back   strands   almost touching   floor   divide
your hair   into three sections   she arched   her back

like a ballerina's   her hair   a waterfall
elbows arrows   pointing   to the ceiling   Miller Science Building

pull from each section   a little at a time   over   under
over   just braid   her hands in my hair   damp

expectant   that morning   every morning   summer of the braid
summer   of my first   quantum entanglement   her mouth

raspberry smear   across   my days

Welcome to Permanence

I always wanted children   I mean
the idea of children I mean

people smiling at my pregnant belly
on the street

My twenty-third summer I rode
the Long Island Railway

into Manhattan every day
the girls on the train I mean women

held their left hands
out into the aisle   their fingers

sparkled I wanted to get married
I mean join their conversation

touch shoulder to shoulder
I mean not be alone

By the end of that summer
I'd lost fifteen pounds   binged

on Saks chocolate
every day   sucked

on the fingers of the third-year associate
delivered a muffin

to the pregnant girl in the stairwell
By the end of that summer

I had the ring   I mean a focal point
the ladies on the train

started saving me a seat
the wedding was planned

I was pregnant I mean the lid
was nailed shut   I mean from the inside

To the River

Feet on the dashboard, knees to her chin. Waits for him to emerge from the woods, zipping his fly. A marriage will grow here, in the light of the speedometer. Truck bed, wool blankets, blue plastic tarp. His thick arm had pinned her like a tree branch after a storm. The sound of the river rushing over rocks, the Big Dipper willing to scoop her away if only she would ask. Instead, Aren't you glad you have me to sleep next to? Turned to him. Held her breath.

There's no mistaking it now, here in the passenger seat. He'd made her wait. Lifted the crane of his arm and sat up. His voice came rough, like bark. Snapped his belt buckle, put his fingers in her hair. Pulled, enough to lift her chin, show her throat. He strides out of the woods now, a wolf. Crouches in the driver's seat. She watches him shield the flame with his cupped hand while he lights a cigarette, then rests a wrist on the steering wheel. Smoke gathers his cheekbones into an arrow pointing down and down and down. Under.

Match

Lit, struck. Made in heaven, made
of wood. Splinter, strike, sulfur, sizzle, snap, slap. Catch.
Fire. Ash. Column, quivering. Cigarette.
Asleep.
Smoker falls, ashes
fall. Catch.
Catch fire. Fire. Flame. Flames
lick. Tongue, tongues,
tongues

of flames lick, center blue, center
orange. Climb curtains, climb
walls, engulf ceiling.
Dance, hours before

we were dancing. Year turning.
After, a cigarette. A struck match,
Where'd you two meet?
Him. Her. Him. Asleep. We fell. *Oh...*
on Match. Lick, licking,

ashes fall, unnoticed,
smolder. Bed, bedspread, floor, drapes, nightdress, towel.
Lighter flicks, catches. We laugh,
run our fingers through the flame. Stop.
Let a blister form,
to remember. Run a finger.

Her. Him. Him. Lamp, lighter, wheel
turns. Snap. Cigarette,
lit. Red tip. We watch. He inhales.
Exhales.

We ignite.

Aubade in Which I Mapped His Fault Lines

In the months after
he'd crossed the country

fifteen, twenty times, his bloody knuckles
didn't scare me. I hungered

for his brokenness. Eyes fixed
on the ceiling, he said,

I've never told anyone
these two things. My fingers mapped

the veins running
the length of his forearm.

I was sent out West
when I was ten. All summer,

chores. All summer, no mother.
The planes of his face

darkened. The worst thing.
A ranch hand, his oiled belt.

My knees in the dirt, his hands
on my head. In that moment I found

his fault lines,
the places he'd shear off

from himself, the fissures
I'd try to press back together.

The other thing, he said,
I was seven.

I kept an atlas
under my pillow, open

to Switzerland. I thought
only doctors lived there,

the ones
who took her away.

When she returned,
she reached for me,

lines running
along her thighs

like roads.
She'd meant to leave.

Bitch, he said,
and turned his back to me.

It would be months
before the slanting August light

would fall
on his beautiful face

at the exact moment
he hissed, again, Bitch—

and illuminated
the roads in my atlas,

roads I would follow
to Switzerland.

Aubade in Which a Memory Arrives

When the cool blue light emitted from the hidden star
Had traveled more than thirty years through galaxies frozen,
Galaxies flaming,

Had bent around planets lush with azure seas,
Planets with saloons lining
Sunken streets,

Had illuminated the powdery mountains and lava-banked rivers
Of that night he kneeled
At the bed,

Its wintry glare threatened to split me
Into twin moons, cast into
Infinite orbit.

It came in through the eyes
Glittering and flashing,
Ten thousand dartfish breaking the mirrored surface.

Aubade in Which an Angel is Present

You might relay the message the rivers and mountains remained
                                                —Carolyn Forché

What is the sound a daughter makes
as she's being choked?

What sound comes, from which one,
when the stepfather removes his hands

from her throat? You won't find me
peering through a fence

in a grainy military reel,
cheekbones jutting,

you won't find my name
in a European field of poppies.

But this account *is not about experiences,*
it is for me the opening

of a wound, the muffling and silence of a decade,
a gathering of utterances

What is the sound of *in ruins, broken*?
I was casted, crutched, silenced…

> *the way back is lost,*
> *the one obsession*

What is the sound of splintering, of the stepfather
shattering the daughter?

> *whoever can cry*
> *should come here*

IV

Starry Messenger

Star-fueled spacecraft
propelled
by steady diet of photons,
fastest object
ever made by humans,
Juno spent two years
looping through
the Solar System
beyond dusty Mars
and our bright blue planet,
obscured by clouds
formed from kicked-off emissions,
then slingshotted past us
with nary a wave,
somersaulting
over two billion miles
of Milky Way
before pirouetting
above Jupiter's clouds,
ducking under
bands of radiation
and entering
the giant planet's swirling
auroras, its haloes
of storming
magnetic fire.
Today Juno
transmits images
of Jupiter's moons—
Io with its molten interior,
icy Europa,
Ganymede, magnetic field,
underground ocean,
Callisto, ancient
and cratered—

Galileo's starry messengers,
symphony
of swirling gases, gases
from which
we came.

Aubade in Which Grace Appears

We were damaged. We hurt people. We were called selfish so many times we figured what the fuck and slid the last piece of steak from our grandmother's plate. We stole pints of rum raisin even though the raisins thawed and spread like sticky insects on our tongues. We took it out on each other, oldest to youngest, until the dog got a bonnet tied so tight his eyes bugged out. We grew up and left that place, refugees—

We acquired husbands, student loans, a penchant for carving letters lightly into our forearms, kittens that kept coming. We left lovers in pick-up trucks to race home and open cans, scratch under wishbone chins. We got therapy. We went for walk after walk after walk in the woods. We filled the sink with hot water and washed dishes every day.

We stacked folding chairs, jiggled our knees when we sat, got sober standing before a chain link fence, pressing our foreheads to the grid. We were sorry and said so, and after a while our wheels ground to a gravelly stop. We didn't know any better. And then we did.

Child, Mother

This child, who started as autumn leaves
blown against the house,

paper crane with a secret code folded inside, dream
from which I believed

I'd awaken, untroubled, to the old landscape—as easily as setting out milk
for stray kittens. This child,

who emerged from my sliced-through womb as flame flickering
in a liminal space, threatening to be extinguished.

When the nurse waiting at the ER doors lifted him
from my arms, I collapsed on the sidewalk,

twigs flattened underfoot, the vibrating ground echoing
my lone beating heart.

Who would teach me
how to be less careless with my life?

Flake

When he shoved the pillow & threw off
the covers, left the bed
in a huff and strode across the room
to lean the length of his six-foot-four
two-hundred-twenty pound body against the dresser
so that reflected in the mirror I saw
the back of his head, the squared-off
hairline the barber had carefully carved
at the base of his skull,
neat and military, the vast span
from shoulder to shoulder—when he said,
quietly, almost to himself
but not really,
I can't believe
you're going to fucking flake out
on me again—
it wasn't that I was any more afraid
then I always was, it wasn't
that I felt I owed him, in particular, my body
or a fuck or whatever,
it was just that a veil lifted
and I saw, in that moment, pulling the sheet
up around my naked self,
the ledger
in all its ballpoint detail—
scrawled columns, additions,
subtractions.

Escape Velocity

oh sean my umbra   here's the problem   the problem

you want to solve   the me   you want to enter

through mouth ear soul   the me you want to fill

to my edges   the edges   you want

to blur   forehead touching forehead   not one lumen   escaping

sean here's the thing   i'm picking me   oh sean

you magnet me   you're a planet   you're gravity

you're married   you're the boss   you press me hard

against your office wall   oh sean

i've reached   disambiguation   you're a speck

i'm a rocket

i illume   i illume   i illume

All the Stories I Ever Told Myself

                                             all the stories

i ever told   myself the woman

         recoils   raccoon carcass around her neck white gloves

            recoils from the sailor his white hat a sun burning in place of a head

his hands grabbing her

        thigh fingers making

indents   all the stories i had ever told myself   about her

                           and how she did not want

to be   kissed

all the stories i had ever told myself   about   how he

                         kissed her anyway

the shutter opened   a millisecond before   but i was sure

 of my story i saw   her shrug her shoulders to her ears   as the shutter opened i

was mad

   at the photographer and the raccoon woman's friend to the left   (was that

              her friend?) laughing with her mouth hanging

                                open

I was mad at the   photographer

                    "exploiter!" i was saying

 in my head   all the stories i ever told myself   were sure the gloved woman

                     did not want

                     did not want

                     did not want

                          to be kissed

Meditation with Starlings and Curling Iron

Outside my window, a flock of starlings alights
in the Hawthorne tree, garnet

rains down, a feast for the taking. Iridescent
black feathers shimmer in unison

against snow-covered ground. Are they preening?
Or just cold? Which one

is most desired?
I own a curling iron for the first time

since seventh grade, can make my hair fall
in loose waves, gather oohs and ahs, a bird

hoarding berries. Hot hiss of heat-scorched strands
recalls winter walks to middle school

with wet head, retractable curling wand
plugged into girls' bathroom wall. How I worshipped

that totem of heat and metal, its sizzle,
its smoke. How I longed for places

to store my fear, nests of stories
I told myself—weighing x pounds,

weighing y pounds. Thirty years on, I twist
my thick, over-washed locks

into submission, touch wand to forehead
and recoil, scattering bobby pins. All at once,

the starlings lift from the ground,
a red welt blooms. Perhaps

a storm is coming, perhaps
a storm has passed.

Blessing for Uncle Alex

Despite your den
filled with model warships
covered in Swastikas,
your rant just yesterday
about The Liberals,
your abiding insistence
that The Blacks were better off,
your deep voice and hulking body,
the worn and dirty NRA cap
flown on your desk
like a Confederate flag,
your refusal to use any pronoun
other than "he,"
the basement arsenal
you brag about daily,
your exhausting,
combative boxer's stance,
crouched and ready
to throw the first punch, always—
I can't help but bless
that small boy
in his grandfather's barroom,
balancing a tray of whiskies
and praying
to make it across the room.

Every Sentient Being

The carcasses have been piling up
All fall—atrophied chipmunk splayed under our kitchen island,

Mouse belly left in its usual corner of the dining room like a miniature
Human stomach, house-wren

Dragged in dead and half feathered, a pile of delicate bones that fit
In the cup of your hand.

A spine, each vertebrae aligned as in life,
Sits in a puddle spewed by the dog at four a.m. onto the rug

And not the towel that you, nearsighted and naked,
Placed under our retching

Animal. Not eating meat, you say, is a discipline. It's a short hop from flesh
To gin. From sobriety to the salty-sweet of just a couple

Margaritas. But lately you've been thinking
About hunting. What makes a man a man? This morning,

The mouse that skittered around our midnight bedroom
Lay nestled in the stiff folds of your work pants—dirt-crusted

From a week of crawling around attics. You slid them on
And still the mouse clung, its microscopic claws

Embedded in canvas. It did not resist when you lifted each paw, placed it gently
On the woodpile. It did not run away. We said, oh, oh—

We wondered whether it would live.

V

Hush

In my dream, it's a music festival kind of summer day
Where all day I think ants are crawling on my feet

But it's only the grass brushing, brushing.
You appear behind me, chest, hips, forearms

Tip me back into your long swallow, slaking,
Slaking. You exhale *I'm here*

Or *you're beautiful* or
What did you say? This morning, your breath's

Kinetic trace still on my neck, I find that overnight—
After months of playing dead—

The cyclamen's waxy, variegated leaves are beginning
A wet unfolding. Within days

Its upswept petals will wave like prayer flags
Strung in the blackened winter window.

Tulips

Today I miss my father, fifty years
past his death, fifty years past
my birth. No—I miss
the idea of my father, a story I conjure
from photos and letters: his Ray Bans,
his motorbike, his splintered English. Today I forgive
my mother—the way she hated the long line
of decapitated tulips in the yard,
the way she laid the Christmas table
with poinsettias and sterling, how she threw open the door
to a gentile stepfather. Today I love
the five a.m. light, the photons themselves, discrete packages
of leaping electrons. Yesterday's summer fuck—
I love it for its sweaty slickness, its earthy lack
of agenda. I love time itself—
how it prevents everything from happening at once.
I love those fearless birds that skitter
courtyards, alighting on tables, generations
churned through time's engine until wildness
has been smoothed
to the flatness of beach rock.
Fifty years on, I still dream a parallel world: Seder plate,
haroset replete with dates and figs, my mother's head dipping low
to light the candles. And in his chair, week's end
weary, tie loosened and shirtsleeves rolled to elbow—
my father telling me to sit still.

Torch Song for Kayla Mueller

Had she lived, she'd know the difference between true
and magnetic north, what *declination* means. She wouldn't fear

the compass's mathematical face, its four lifesaving directions,
needle a quivering blade—earth's coded truth.

She'd know man or bear might appear and still, she'd turn
her attention to staking her tent, gathering tinder

to coax the first licks of flame
from the forest.

She'd carry her own knife,
fire starter, tweezers, duct tape, safety whistle, map—

she'd always be prepared
for who might come. Unafraid, she'd spend the night alone

among the black flies and wild blueberries, calculate the angle
of the fallen sun. She'd walk with strength

ungendered, as if her twinned world existed,
as if she'd conjured it.

Forest Aubade

The answer: it breaks your heart
                                        every single day
                                        every single day
            you wake up
                    dream-mended, the measured cadence
                    of your love's sawing breath
                    like trail blazes gashed red on trees:
                                        the way through
                        is here
                                and yes you must
                                            keep walking.

Twiggy lines at the corners of your eyes deepen
                                        every single day
                                        every single day
            silver
            threading through your hair gains purchase
            like hooves gripping mountainside:
                                            you must follow
                            the cairns
                                    don't stop no matter
                                            the blistering.

Free moments, start to gather
                                        every single day
                                        every single day
            little bits of forest:
                    needles, cones, the tiniest bird-like branches. Lift sticks
                    from the path:
                                        you must stuff
                        your pockets
                                with each night's warmth.

You'll be astonished
                how quickly
                        it burns.

Aubade in Which I Learn a Biology Lesson

The mom next-door says of her husband, *He hates trees.*
We look up at the maples, their paddles

of leaves. A few feet away, the compost bin churns. Coffee grounds,
kale stems, delicate shells of chickens. My book says, *death*

is just your cells, less organized. Carrot tops,
onion skin, deflated tomato. August, and the great pine

in my front yard opens its arms to the whole street. Sticky yellow pollen
finds its way into all the houses,

turning the keys of my neighbor's piano to sunshine. Needles,
lilac husks, scent of dirt

and winter. This morning, a great buzzing
interrupts my dream. From the window, I watch a waltz:

chainsaw and tree, amputation of branches. The laying out
of the body, the gathering of men.

Gaping hole like a tooth missing. Sky.

Physics Lesson For Those in Despair

the president lies   i used to lie   my lies   made my world
a place   where my synapses   thankfully
could keep   firing   in formation   with the story
my mother told herself   the president's   lies
keep us   entombed
in a reality   tilted   to steady
him   quantum physics theorizes   we are
but a hologram   thinnest edge   coating   projection
that which can't be   sensed
through the   human   body
my stylist   erasing my grays   tells her   christmas eve
story   her brother's girlfriend   died
in his arms   will your brother use again
i ask   when the president   lies
we shake   our heads in private bow our heads
when he enters   the boardroom
quantum physics   predicts   that all possible scenarios
occur   simultaneously   an atom
can be overwhelmed   by fentanyl-laced
heroin   and in a parallel   universe can   toast
the new year   so perhaps   the president's lie
is true
somewhere   perhaps   one fold   in time
to the left   the ocean
we surfed in may
without wetsuits   is cooling   and those deniers
have whirled   through galaxies
and seen   the truth   perhaps
the president has

Inventory

My father didn't die when I was an infant.
We didn't spend the summers at the ocean.
I didn't spend my time there underwater.
The house I grew up in didn't have flowerboxes.
My imaginary friend Spirit didn't live in the mirror.
I didn't play soccer in college.
I wasn't destined for the Olympics in judo.
I didn't tutor Mike Tyson.
My mother didn't cremate my father's body.
My Israeli grandparents didn't blame [me] [her].
I didn't get stoned for the first time at twelve.
I didn't trade sex for Coach bags with my first husband.
My first fuck wasn't [by] [with] my stepfather.
My second fuck wasn't [by] [with] my judo coach.
My friend's father didn't go down on me while his wife got high
    in the next room.
They didn't have a pinball machine in their house.
I [don't] love my mother.
I didn't get on a bus in the middle of the night in Leningrad
    with two Russian boys.
They didn't love me for my Marlboros.
I haven't had [three] [five] [zero] abortions.
I wasn't dissociated for thirty years
and didn't re-inhabit my body one asana at a time.
I didn't major in Chemistry to punish myself.
I didn't spend thirteen years in therapy.
I'm not lucky to be alive, twenty times over.
I'm not terrified every day.
I'm not a miracle.
I [wasn't] [was] loved.

If Anything Happened

She'd get rid of it,
he says. His first
older woman, he loves
her wild hair, her way
with a microphone.
We drive through
mountains ablaze
with late October, riot
of red and reflection,
humming miles
ticking through
his worry.
She must go back
home, to Spain
at the end
of the semester.
She lost her mom
last year, breast
cancer.
They were close.
Is she on the pill?
She's a huge fan
of yours, she says
that any mother
who raised a man
like me must
be good.

I got rid of it.
My first serious
boyfriend, I loved
watching his wet hair
dry to blonde.
We drove
to Planned Parenthood,
diesel smell
of city and winter.
He counted twenties
at the counter.
I never asked
how he got his mom's
car, the money,
what thrashing
awaited him at the end
of that day.
Sitting before
the exhausted nurse—
She's gotta go
on the pill, honey.
You gotta keep her
warm on the way home,
honey. He did,
heat cranked high.
I never told
my mother.

My mother got rid
of it. Her first
married man, her
father's white-knuckle
midnight speeding.
She drove me
to college, through
landscape raked
with skeletal trees.
Her father threw
an arm around
the doctor, she waited
outside their circle.
She had no choice.
She would dissolve,
banished
for months. Alone
in the stirrups—
no nurse to hold her hand.
Where was your mother?
No pill, then.
It would have killed
my mother, she says.
You're the first person
I've told.
I remember being so cold
on the way home.

Make a Law That Loves the One Who Breaks it

make pipes under sidewalks hot with steam   sidewalks slick with dripping
slush   grocery carts whose wheels chew through snow   tracks
that lead to lighted tents that glow   let hospice workers feel safe enough
to visit   make the son keeper of the morphine   let his father pick
through encampments cursing   let him shine a light in tent after tent
  make the city scatter coats and batteries   let the father lead
the clean up effort
    make shelter-garden show hyacinth and crocus   let reporters document
first purples   and photographers lie eye to eye with papery blooms
let the gardener show her blackened grin   and her husband be drunk
  and crush the green
        let the cop have gotten laid that morning   let his cheeks retain
their highest glow   make him dream the mother of his children
  let him step lightly through the tulips   ignore smashed glass
and scattered needles   let mercy settle in like march mist   let the father
be the first one home   let no one hear him say   so today's the day
let the corpse be cold and all alone   let the daughter take gymnastics
and the late bus   let the story be the waiting
        and the not knowing   make a law that prostrates itself at the feet
of luck   let there be no audience that day   let the one moon shine
in star-pricked sky   let it reflect in a hundred puddles

Where Rivers and Mountains Remain

Kayla I know I'm imagining you
I have nothing to ask for don't worry
If you want to Kayla step into my dream
Where rivers and mountains remain

I'll ask for nothing Kayla
If you want to come stay in this house
Rivers and mountains just outside the window
Kayla come join me in jacks

I'll leave the door open for you
Is there anything you need to say
Jacks are here waiting stacked on the floor
The sun has been asking for you

My sister you can tell me everything
Kayla I honor your wild
There's a column of sunlight marking the way for you
And the invisible moon waits above

Kayla I honor your wild
You've done more than your share you can rest
The moon waits she'll rock you tonight
I wish for you silvery dreams

Kayla you can rest
Come sit and I'll braid your hair
You'll be beautiful in your dreams tonight
Here's a crown woven from stars

Come sit and I'll untangle your hair
I gathered these stars so you'll always have light
Rivers and mountains remain such beauty
Kayla I know I'm imagining you

Praise Planet: Galactic Ballet

after Gabrielle Calvocoressi

Physics, specifically quantum. The idea
that ideas are chemical reactions
sparking between neurons. That
we think we know everything
and then: we don't know
anything. And beginning again.
That emptiness is the opposite
of nothingness. His animal
swagger after fifteen pull-ups
dangling a twenty-five-pound weight
from a chain around his waist.
The perfect kale salad spiked
with mint. A new possibility:
my dead father has been here
all along, just less organized.
That time is a label we fix
to our perception of change.
Ross Gay's father peering
through the cathedral-window skin
of a newly grown plum.
That atoms are not things,
but events. And Orion, his bow,
his belt: galactic ballet. And photons—
oh, photons. Scrape of graphite
against steel, the near-spark,
preparing for a morning
of drawing. That if electrons
didn't agree to swap, Oprah
wouldn't exist. My niece,
in constant motion, phenomena
of humanity. Warming
my tea mug with hot water
like my grandmother did.
And epigenetics, stories that divide

and multiply, frantic charge
into the next generation.
That climate change has afforded us
crystalline-prism snow
instead of the usual New England
ice. A run of weeks
of minus nine degrees
Fahrenheit. Snap of clarity
and then gone. That thermometers exist
and give us a feeling of agency.
The dog parting snow
like Jesus, shoulder-deep, racing
toward the reward
of cheese. And cheese, miracle
of ancient alchemy. That time
is how we measure motion,
the vibration of a quark or Earth's
rotation. That we can choose
where to put our attention,
which dog to feed. Meditation, stilling
the mind. And all the books
explaining how to do it. And paper,
the turn of a page.
That Buddhism and physics
agree: nothing can start
nor cease to exist.
That we don't have to plan
to breathe. That neither
do trees.

Authentic Presence
—after Chogyam Trungpa

The dragon breathes out lightning and roars out thunder. That brings the rain.

>   I watch my neighbor's son dive and surface,
>   dive and surface in the backyard pool I keep up
>   just for him. Seven or eight, he has home-sheared bangs
>   like my brother's in a school picture from the 70s. The boy
>   sees me watching him, offers a tiny wave, goes under.
>   Away in the city, too far for gathering in, my son
>   has diagnosed himself manic.

The tiger walks slowly through the jungle. It swims through ferns and vines like a
wave.

>   Whose time in the tangle is so smooth
>   it feels like swimming, parting the lush green stroke
>   by stroke? My jungle years were dark,
>   damp—something fetid grew in that place. A madman
>   trailed me mile after mile. Many days, I felt his breath
>   on my neck. When at last I took to the trees,
>   caught a glimpse of vast sky, the madman
>   kept right on running. To him, I was leaf.

The snow lion roams the highlands, where the atmosphere is clear and the air is
fresh.

>   My brother at eleven swings his bat—ping!
>   Aluminum meets leather, white speck
>   sails skyward. This morning, my psychiatrist friend
>   posts photo after photo of bright red birds
>   looking at themselves in a mirror, preening

in their bath. They never get tired
of their own fascination, he says.

Their actions are always beautiful and dignified.

> My brother turns thirteen, stashes a pipe
> under his mattress, smashes empty fifths of vodka
> against the stadium fence. What do I want? The end
> of needles, bottles. To have spotted my brother out there,
> at sea, to have hauled him, stroke by stroke,
> out of deep water, dragged him to shore.
> My neighbor's boy, splashing in the pool—
> what will his body become?

The closed and poverty-stricken world begins to fall apart.

> James Baldwin: He was Sonny's witness
> that deep water and drowning
> were not the same thing.
> Maybe my son is manic, maybe
> he's just having a life.

Earth is my witness. I touch Earth, touch ground.

> We walk through the woods,
> my neighbor's son holds treats for the dog
> in his pocket. Rain rests
> on each leaf. The dog barks, the boy
> smacks a branch. Suddenly,
> we're soaked.

What Bright Freedom Lies Here

What bright freedom lies here, at the tail end
of forty years of bleeding, forty years of praying?
Please don't let me be, please let me be...
In last night's dream I thought I was losing
my hair—I kept checking. And the night before,
waves breaking in my body at 2 a.m. How will I die?
And what would it feel like to shave my head,
letting hairbands, braids, shampoo
wash out with the tide?

For forty years, I've risen and fallen
on the swell of hormones: migraines, aching wrists,
three pounds, five pounds. Tissue paper touched
to cervix each month, pink smear to sudden flow.
In this new quiet I hear the echo of four decades:
*PMS, condoms, pulsating uterus, breasts (oh breasts!),
pregnant, not pregnant, hum, hum, hum.*

The first time I bled: Halloween. Twelve and a half,
I was a bunny in a flannel sleeper. Saw the blood—
no, no, no, no, no! Shame like a tidal wave: this metallic
intimacy, this garnet vulnerability. And so it became
my familiar, *hum, hum, hum,* and the men
chatting me up at gas stations, in airports,
on the ferry to Belfast...

What bright freedom lies here? The storm
has stopped raging, the wind has died down,
the moon illuminates white sand.
Detritus rests quietly: driftwood, hollow shell
of horseshoe crab. No longer a child, no longer
in captivity. Today, I'll walk straight
into the wind.

Notes

"Leap" is based on a family photo circa 1971.

"Dear Kayla, Did You Pray." Kayla Mueller was an American, "[d]escribed by friends and family members as a deeply idealistic young woman eager to help those less fortunate. Ms. Mueller was just shy of her 25th birthday on Aug. 4, 2013, when she disappeared in the northern Syrian city of Aleppo. She had arrived in Syria a day earlier with a Syrian man who has been described as her boyfriend or colleague." https://www.nytimes.com/2015/02/11/world/middleeast/parents-of-kayla-mueller-isis-hostage-confirm-she-is-dead.html

Around September 2014, Kayla was "handed over to Abu Sayyaf, and his sadistic wife, Umm Sayyaf—Tunisians who kept the American and a half-dozen Yazidi girls as sex slaves for ISIS 'Caliph' Abu Bakr al-Baghdadi…'Baghdadi took her several times in the night for himself,' Yazidi hostage Julia recounted, noting that Mueller would return later and try not to cry, though at times she broke down. [Kayla] told the girls that part of surviving was being forced to pretend she had converted to Islam so the ISIS leader could sexually assault her, though she still clung secretly to her Christian faith." http://abcnews.go.com/International/kayla-mueller-captivity-courage-selflessness-defended-christian-faith/story?id=41626763

"Dear Beauty Editor" is based on the column in the Girl Scouting magazine, *American Girl*, circa 1978.

"Things Said to a Teenage Girl at the Dojo." "Over the course of two decades, at least 368 gymnasts have alleged they were sexually assaulted or exploited by adults working in the sport." *NPR, December 15, 2016*

"Dear Kayla, Did You Sleep." Kayla passed up a chance to escape in the fall of 2014 in order to protect the young Yazidi girls who were being held in captivity with her. "Julia [one of the Yazidi girls] revealed in a '20/20' interview how Mueller—who was frequently raped by [ISIS Caliph] al-Baghdadi—passed up a chance at an escape in order to increase the odds for the Yazidi teens, who were able to sneak out of the ISIS kingpin's house late one night in a flight to freedom. 'I told Kayla, "We want to escape," and I asked her to come with us. She told me, "No, because I am American. If I escape with you, they will do everything to find us again,"' Julia said. 'It is better for you to escape alone. I will stay here,' Mueller said, according to Julia." http://abcnews.go.com/International/kayla-mueller-captivity-courage-selflessness-defended-christian-faith/story?id=41626763

"The Body Keeps the Score" take its title from *The Body Keeps the Score: Brain, Body and Mind in the Healing of Trauma* by Bessel Van der Kolk, M.D.

"Summer of the Braid" is for Dr. Julie Staley, 1965-2008 and is after the poet Meaghan Quinn.

"Welcome to Permanence" owes its structure to Morgan Parker's poem, *Welcome to the Jungle*.

"Tel Aviv." The line "there is a sadness everywhere present" is from Jennifer Grotz's poem, *Poppies*.

"Aubade in Which an Angel is Present" is for Carolyn Forché. "Poem as trace, poem as evidence." The italicized lines are from the forward to the poetry anthology *Against Forgetting*, edited by Carolyn Forché.

"Starry Messenger" depicts the voyage of the Juno spacecraft, which sent back its first images from Jupiter in July 2016.

"Escape Velocity." In physics, escape velocity is the minimum speed needed for an object to escape from the gravitational influence of a massive body. https://en.wikipedia.org/wiki/Escape_velocity

"All the Stories I Ever Told Myself" nods to Joan Didion. "We tell ourselves stories in order to live."

"Make a Law That Loves the One Who Breaks It" takes its title from Larry Levis's poem, *Make a Law So That the Spine Remembers Wings*.

"Where Rivers and Mountains Remain." Kayla died on or around February 6, 2015. "For one tortured weekend, the parents of Kayla Mueller refused to believe that their daughter was dead. From their home in Prescott, Ariz., they issued an impassioned plea to the Islamic State, which had held her captive since August 2013, and urged the extremist organization to contact them privately with proof of her death. The militants acquiesced and sent at least three photographs of her corpse." https://www.nytimes.com/2015/02/11/world/middleeast/parents-of-kayla-mueller-isis-hostage-confirm-she-is-dead.html?_r=0

"Praise Planet: Galactic Ballet" was inspired by Gabrielle Calvocoressi's poem, *Praise House: The New Economy* and Ross Gay's poem, *The Opening*.

The italicized lines in "Authentic Presence" are from *Shambala, The Sacred Path of the Warrior* by Chogyam Trungpa. "[D]eep water and drowning were not the same thing," are from *Sonny's Blues* by James Baldwin.

A note on the cover art:
The cover painting was made in 1963 by the author's father, Menashe Sofer. An Iraqi Jew who was displaced from Baghdad in 1949, along with his family, he was among the first Israeli settlers, sent to live and work on a kibbutz at age 13. He met the author's mother, an American, in Tel Aviv in 1960, and emigrated to the United States once married, where he was an art major at the University of Michigan, Ann Arbor. He died in 1966 at 28 years old, when the author was less than a year old. The cover painting is the only surviving painting of the many he made. The others burned in a house fire.

Erica Bodwell is a poet, attorney and visual artist. She is the author of the chapbook *Up Liberty Street*, and her work appears in many journals including Beloit, PANK, Apiary and HEART. She is the mother of two grown sons and lives with her husband and two dogs in Concord, New Hampshire. In addition to her day job as a healthcare lawyer, she raised more than a million dollars for civil legal aid in New Hampshire, which overwhelmingly serves the needs of women and children. *Crown of Wild* is her first full-length collection.

Publications by Two Sylvias Press:

The Daily Poet: Day-By-Day Prompts For Your Writing Practice
by Kelli Russell Agodon and Martha Silano (Print and eBook)

The Daily Poet Companion Journal (Print)

Fire On Her Tongue: An Anthology of Contemporary Women's Poetry
edited by Kelli Russell Agodon and Annette Spaulding-Convy (Print and eBook)

The Poet Tarot and Guidebook: A Deck Of Creative Exploration (Print)

Crown of Wild, Winner of the 2018 Two Sylvias Press Wilder Prize
by Erica Bodwell (Print)

American Zero, Winner of the 2018 Two Sylvias Press Chapbook Prize
by Stella Wong (Print and eBook)

The Inspired Poet: Writing Exercises to Spark New Work
by Susan Landgraf (Print)

All Transparent Things Need Thundershirts, Winner of the 2017 Two Sylvias
Press Wilder Prize
by Dana Roeser (Print and eBook)

Where The Horse Takes Wing: The Uncollected Poems of Madeline DeFrees
edited by Anne McDuffie (Print and eBook)

In The House Of My Father, Winner of the 2017 Two Sylvias Press Chapbook
Prize by Hiwot Adilow (Print and eBook)

Box, Winner of the 2017 Two Sylvias Press Poetry Prize
by Sue D. Burton (Print and eBook)

Tsigan: The Gypsy Poem (New Edition)
by Cecilia Woloch (Print and eBook)

PR For Poets
by Jeannine Hall Gailey (Print and eBook)

Appalachians Run Amok, Winner of the 2016 Two Sylvias Press Wilder Prize
by Adrian Blevins (Print and eBook)

Pass It On!
by Gloria J. McEwen Burgess (Print)

Killing Marias
by Claudia Castro Luna (Print and eBook)

The Ego and the Empiricist, Finalist 2016 Two Sylvias Press Chapbook Prize
by Derek Mong (Print and eBook)

The Authenticity Experiment
by Kate Carroll de Gutes (Print and eBook)

Mytheria, Finalist 2015 Two Sylvias Press Wilder Prize
by Molly Tenenbaum (Print and eBook)

Arab in Newsland , Winner of the 2016 Two Sylvias Press Chapbook Prize
by Lena Khalaf Tuffaha (Print and eBook)

The Blue Black Wet of Wood, Winner of the 2015 Two Sylvias Press Wilder Prize
by Carmen R. Gillespie (Print and eBook)

Fire Girl: Essays on India, America, and the In-Between
by Sayantani Dasgupta (Print and eBook)

Blood Song
by Michael Schmeltzer (Print and eBook)

Naming The No-Name Woman,
Winner of the 2015 Two Sylvias Press Chapbook Prize
by Jasmine An (Print and eBook)

Community Chest
by Natalie Serber (Print)

Phantom Son: A Mother's Story of Surrender
by Sharon Estill Taylor (Print and eBook)

What The Truth Tastes Like
by Martha Silano (Print and eBook)

landscape/heartbreak
by Michelle Peñaloza (Print and eBook)

Earth, Winner of the 2014 Two Sylvias Press Chapbook Prize
by Cecilia Woloch (Print and eBook)

The Cardiologist's Daughter
by Natasha Kochicheril Moni (Print and eBook)

She Returns to the Floating World
by Jeannine Hall Gailey (Print and eBook)

Hourglass Museum
by Kelli Russell Agodon (eBook)

Cloud Pharmacy
by Susan Rich (eBook)

Dear Alzheimer's: A Caregiver's Diary & Poems
by Esther Altshul Helfgott (eBook)

Listening to Mozart: Poems of Alzheimer's
by Esther Altshul Helfgott (eBook)

Crab Creek Review 30th Anniversary Issue featuring Northwest Poets
edited by Kelli Russell Agodon and Annette Spaulding-Convy (eBook)

Please visit Two Sylvias Press (www.twosylviaspress.com) for information on purchasing our print books, eBooks, writing tools, and for submission guidelines for our annual book prizes.

The Wilder Series Poetry Book Prize

The Wilder Series Book Prize is an annual contest hosted by Two Sylvias Press. It is open to women over 50 years of age (established or emerging poets) and includes a $1000 prize, publication by Two Sylvias Press, 20 copies of the winning book, and a vintage, art nouveau pendant. Women submitting manuscripts may be poets with one or more previously published chapbooks/books or poets without any prior chapbook/book publications. The judges for the prize are Two Sylvias Press cofounders and coeditors, Kelli Russell Agodon and Annette Spaulding-Convy.

The Wilder Series Book Prize draws its inspiration from American author, Laura Ingalls Wilder, who published her first *Little House* book at age 65 and completed the last manuscript in the series at age 76. Wilder's autobiography, which she wrote in her late 60s, was published in 2014, after having been rejected in the 1930s by editors due to its "inappropriate" and "mature" material. Two Sylvias Press is proud to introduce a poetry series featuring women over age 50—young women may be wild, but mature women are *wilder.*

To learn more about submitting to the Wilder Prize, please visit: http://twosylviaspress.com/wilder-series-poetry-book-prize.html

The Wilder Series Book Prize Winners and Finalists

2018:
Erica Bodwell, *Crown of Wild* (Winner)

2017:
Dana Roeser, *All Transparent Things Need Thundershirts* (Winner)

2016:
Adrian Blevins, *Appalachians Run Amok* (Winner)

2015:
Carmen R. Gillespie, *The Blue Black Wet of Wood* (Winner)
Molly Tenenbaum, *Mytheria* (Finalist)

CPSIA information can be obtained
at www.ICGtesting.com
Printed in the USA
FSHW011212171220
76817FS